*in search of the*

# GOOD LIFE

# CHARLES COLSON

WITH HAROLD FICKETT

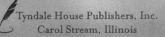

Tyndale House Publishers, Inc.
Carol Stream, Illinois

Visit Tyndale's exciting Web site at www.tyndale.com

*TYNDALE* is a registered trademark of Tyndale House Publishers, Inc.

Tyndale's quill logo is a trademark of Tyndale House Publishers, Inc.

*In Search of the Good Life*

Designed by Jessie McGrath

Scripture quotations are taken from the *Holy Bible*, New International Version ®. NIV ®. Copyright © 1973, 1978, 1984 by International Bible Society. Used by permission of Zondervan Publishing House. All rights reserved.

ISBN-13: 978-1-4143-1130-2
ISBN-10: 1-4143-1130-3

Printed in the United States of America

12   11   10   09   08   07   06
7    6    5    4    3    2    1

# INTRODUCTION

What makes life worth living? Why am I here? What's my purpose? Can I really live a meaningful life?

Through the busyness of life, these questions weave in and out of the daily grind. In his book *The Good Life*, Chuck Colson challenges us to step back from the pressures of our fast-moving, high-tech world and face these important questions.

One day we seem to have things under control; the next day we get steamrollered by events. Life is messy, confusing, filled with paradoxes. Yet Colson reminds us that in the midst of the uncertainty and chaos of our lives, truth about what matters can be found only if we take the quest for truth seriously.

How we answer life's big questions determines how our lives unfold.

**LIFE IS GOOD. I'VE ACHIEVED**
everything I've always wanted—and
then some. I have more money than
I need, a penthouse overlooking
Central Park, and a luxury yacht. But
I still wonder if something is missing.
Is there more?

—CEO OF NEW YORK FORTUNE 500 COMPANY

---

*Not all of us are jet-set executives or famous.
Often we read the stories about those people in
glossy magazines, and we feel on the outside
of the club of people who have achieved "the
good life." Chuck Colson points out that those
magazine stories usually present only one side
of the story . . .*

---

Can being a rich corporate executive really
give life meaning? Mounting evidence suggests
that the answer is a resounding no. At the end
of the day, even after high-powered meetings,
the closing of a lucrative business deal, or the

purchase of a second dream home, there remains an unshakable reminder in the soul of humanity that life still feels empty. The truth is, life might be better in the twenty-first century, but we somehow feel worse.

Like no other generation, Americans today enjoy their wealth. Theorist James B. Twitchell defends consumerism as a belief system that says, "I found it, I am saved." Somewhere along the way we stopped looking for a salvation experience in church and found it at the mall. Back in the 1950s, C. S. Lewis, the great apologist and Oxford don, wrote to a young skeptic, "You say the materialist universe is ugly. . . . If you are really a product of the materialistic universe, how is it you don't feel at home there?"[1] Today, Lewis's question still rings true to us. Our dream job doesn't quite satisfy our quest for success. Our new luxury condominium doesn't quite feel like the *right* home. Why?

Paradoxically, striving for possessions and status, the things we think will bring us the happy ending, actually can strip meaning from our lives. The belief system that tells us spending and acquiring will bring us satisfaction often erodes our human dignity. Materialism says having an important position or living in the right neighborhood is really what makes our lives valuable. We are nothing more than what we consume. Ultimately, materialism neglects what it means to be truly human, to be people created in the image of God. Our worth is found not in what we do but in who we are.

Of course, there is nothing wrong with having goals, working hard, and improving life for our families. I've always been ambitious and have had a tremendous drive to succeed. I won a scholarship to college and was determined to make it big. Most of us hope to be better off financially in ten years than we are now. Most of us want to work toward a promotion, not a demotion. We naturally want to give our children and families better opportunities than we had growing up. Progress is a part of our testimony as Americans. But progress cannot be the end goal or ideal for our lives. Rather it is a comparative tool we can use, not a measuring stick that determines if we have found the good life.

Modern thinkers have made materialism the basis for an entire worldview. Many of us have bought into the "myth of progress," which teaches that history is moving toward an earthly utopia. If we can just become better, smarter, and more efficient people, we will evolve to be a greater society. Every job or thing we do should be a step up on the ladder of success. In other words, humanity can be spared from life's woes if we continue to pursue progress.

But the natural order of life seems to prove otherwise. Look at the evidence around us. Let's say you are a CEO who has achieved the job of a lifetime. It takes only a few hours at the office to realize that the job is not perfect, and neither are you. No one can deny that people make mistakes. Because we are imperfect people, our jobs are also imperfect. We were created for more than just the physical world we can see and touch. Think for a moment about some of the high-profile corporate tycoons in the media. Do you really believe that living in palaces, drinking expensive wine, and having millions in the bank have given them peace?

Although the consumerism voice in our culture entices us to indulge in all we desire, something inherent in us tells us we were created to partake in something higher, a higher purpose. In *The Good Life*, I point out this real struggle we all have: Our higher nature wants to pursue a higher purpose, and our lower nature wants to satisfy our selfish pleasures. The good life is often thought to be simply living for pleasure and acquiring possessions and goods. Maybe you are dreaming of the new BMW you think will make life perfect. The truth is, we know that once we purchase such a thrill, the actual pleasure is never as great as once anticipated. In reality, the excitement turns out to be pretty short-lived.

This insatiable desire in us, that unquenchable thirst, points to the natural order of life. Pleasure isn't enough, and in the end it doesn't make us happy. To find the good life, we need a creed that transcends self, a sense of significance that reaches beyond our jobs, and a life that is pursued beyond the physical world of materialism.

**I'M UP TO MY EARS IN DEBT!
I can't ever get ahead. My only hope is
to win the lottery. That would solve all
my problems.**—Detroit homeowner

---

*Many of us are simply trying to eke out a comfortable existence while dealing with rising costs in housing, education, and fuel. How many times have you caught yourself fantasizing about a windfall the way the homeowner does? In* The Good Life, *Colson explores why these fantasies are so alluring—and yet so illusory.*

---

The winning numbers were 10-25-38-39-50 with a Mega Ball 12. Sixty-seven-year-old Geraldine Williams just happened to pick the winning numbers. Her odds of winning: 1 in 135,145,920. Williams, used to having a feather duster and a mop in hand, now held the winning ticket. This hardworking cleaning woman stepped forward to claim her $294 million jackpot, one of the largest jackpots ever to go to a single person. Such a story warms the heart and increases our own determination to try and beat the odds ourselves. We find ourselves wondering, *If I just had a million dollars . . .*

One-half of the American adult population spends $45 billion annually on 35,000 lottery games in 40 states, plus the District of Columbia, Puerto Rico, and the U.S. Virgin Islands.[2] That's a lot of money when you consider that you have a better chance of being struck by lightning than of winning the jackpot.

Money isn't evil, however. Some of my friends have acquired vast wealth in their lifetime. But the happiest people I know are those who are not controlled by their wealth. In other words, if the money were gone tomorrow, their lives would still have purpose and significance. One such friend is Dois Rosser, an automobile dealer from Virginia. Using money from a ministry he started with his own funds, he has helped build churches all around the globe.

After a recent trip Dois gathered his family to discuss his estate plans. He gave an opportunity for each family member to claim his or her inheritance, but unanimously they all donated theirs back to Rosser's foundation. Not only has Dois proved that money does not control his life, but he has also passed that important legacy on to his family. The Rosser family knows that materialism is not the goal.

Like Geraldine Williams, most working-class, lotto-playing people have felt the burdens of financial stress. It's easy to believe that life would be completely carefree if money were no object. But over the years, research has confirmed that money really can't buy happiness. In case after case of lottery winners, life's problems continue. Some winners have become recluses, some lose their money to scam artists, and some end up in despair.

Why didn't the winning ticket buy happiness in such cases? Well, I believe some of these unhappy winners tried to use money as the answer to life's big questions: Why am I here? What am I doing? Does my life matter? Wealth, power, and success are means we can put to good use, but they were never meant to be an end in themselves. Money can't solve life's dilemmas.

Consumerism sees wealth as the key to open the door of opportunity. Such a belief system puts our humanity at risk. But something within tells us that our value comes from being part of the human race. Because we have a divine Creator, our lives have far more worth than our bank accounts. Simply satisfying our debts or acquiring assets falls short of what this life is really all about. We were never meant to place our faith in the gods of chance and fortune. Rather, we were born with a God-given purpose that carries us along, each day attesting to our infinite worth.

**I LOVE STUDYING POLITICS.**
**But once I get out of school, will I really**
**be able to make a difference in society**
**and change some of the wrongs in my**
**own community?**

—POLITICAL SCIENCE MAJOR

—•◦•—

*We all yearn for significance. Our desire to*
*make a difference in the world emerges as we*
*pursue education, make career choices, and*
*try to undo what we've messed up in our lives.*
*What answers about your own worth are you*
*still seeking? Whether you are a college student*
*or an ex-con, Chuck Colson points to the eter-*
*nal value individual lives can hold.*

—•◦•—

I've always been idealistic, and when I was
young, I had big dreams for myself. During
World War II, I organized an effort that raised
enough money to buy the army a Jeep. As
young as I was, I saw that little efforts could
go a long way. My desire to make a difference

II

later led me not only to join the Marines but also to enter the world of politics. What drew me to politics was not just power but the desire to really change society. I wanted to learn all that I could and contribute in some way to my country.

Young people today have so many different opportunities to have an impact on their generation and even generations to come. Every life is significant, and more important, each life is significant to God. Although I was a conscientious man during my years in the White House, I really didn't understand what true significance meant until after I entered prison. My soul-searching began behind bars as I realized I had confused fame and power with significance. As I did menial prison work, I learned that work—any work—can be significant and satisfying. And it was in prison, challenged by my fellow inmates not to forget them when I left, that I found my most significant work—giving myself for others.

The longer I live, the more I realize the impact that just one life can have on society. Never underestimate what one life can do. Take, for example, the life of William Wilberforce. Two hundred years ago, he led the campaign to end the British slave trade, forever changing his country. Wilberforce, too, struggled with this question: What should I do with my life?

In his younger years Wilberforce was set on pursuing a successful career in politics. A wealthy and popular young man, he enjoyed life to the fullest: dinners, balls, and roguish activity with friends. But after he became a Christian, his worldview radically changed. He found himself questioning how he should spend the remainder of his time and talents. At first he thought he might be called to be a clergyman, but a good minister friend, John Newton, talked him out of it. Newton saw that Wilberforce had tremendous gifts and talents in the area of politics and that he could use his public life to shape the hearts of the British people.

Realizing that the opportunities before him were divinely orchestrated, Wilberforce continued on as a member of Parliament, and God used him to abolish slavery in Great Britain and to bring about dramatic changes in the culture of England. His concern for others—whether stranger or neighbor, slave or free—came from his biblical worldview. Wilberforce used his life to make a difference in his world.

Sometimes we forget to look at the factors right under our noses. What natural skills do you have? How can you use them to help others? When I was growing up, I thought the goal was to rise from my modest beginnings, earn lots of money, and have a comfortable retirement. I now understand that such a dream was terribly hollow and flat. I now understand that life can have value, that we can make a difference well beyond what we do during our lifetime.

Not all of us will be called to the public square as Wilberforce was, but we all are artisans who can contribute truth and beauty to society through work well done. Everyone has something to offer society. Once we are able to grasp our inherent worth, our lives naturally lead us to where we can make this world a better place.

**I'M UP FOR PAROLE THIS YEAR,**
but I'm scared to get out and make a way
for myself. How could any good ever
come from the mess I've made of
my life? I can't undo what I've done.

—INCARCERATED FELON, STATE PENITENTIARY

———

*Maybe you aren't a felon, but you feel as if
you've really made a mess of your life in some
way. God has given us free will. We all have the
freedom to make choices. Perhaps you feel as if
you've squandered all that was good in your
life. You may feel that life is really over for you
and nothing can undo what you've done. If so,
you have something in common with former
presidential aide Chuck Colson. Read his story,
and see the significance he found in the lowest
of places.*

———

On July 8, 1974, four U.S. marshals picked me
up to take me to prison. I thought all I had
worked for was lost. For months my name had

been mired in the Watergate scandal. I was no longer the big-time White House hatchet man. I was just a felon. I had pleaded guilty to obstruction of justice and was sentenced to three years in prison. My world had collapsed. I never dreamed I would be able to do anything significant with my life.

But paradoxically, prison was one of the best things that ever happened to me. In prison I realized that success, power, achievement, and fame are worthless. They are empty, meaningless. My only meaning came from knowing that I belonged to God.

I thank God for Watergate. It wasn't until I was stripped of all I knew to be the good life that I was confronted with the reality of one of life's greatest paradoxes: Out of suffering and defeat often comes victory.

Perhaps you are in a place of defeat and suffering. While I don't want to suggest that trials or suffering magically transform us, I do believe that earth-shattering experiences can help open our eyes to reality. Crises can show us what we are really made of.

Soviet writer and dissident Aleksandr Solzhenitsyn wrote, "Bless you, prison. Bless you for being in my life, for there, lying on the rotting prison floor, I came to realize that the object of life is not prosperity, as we are made to believe, but the maturing of the human soul."[3] In my nine-by-twelve cell, I found this to be profoundly true. God was molding me to be the man He intended.

As a result of my time in prison, God gave me the most meaningful and satisfying experience of my life—ministering to prisoners all around the world. I've been in more than six hundred different prisons, some of the worst hellholes imaginable. Working in prison ministry is demanding, full of constant pressure. My life has even been threatened. But I've never looked back. I know God redeemed me from the prison cells of my own heart and gave me a reason to start over.

I am living proof that God can redeem any life, no matter how hopeless. What I do today is an expression of my gratitude to God. He took the worst experience of my life and profoundly redeemed it.

**I WAS JUST OFFERED AN**
administrative position with the school
district. It pays 30 percent more than
my teaching job, and I sure could use
the money. But I know my students need
hope to keep them off the streets. My
friends say I would be crazy to turn down
the admin job. I'm torn.

—INNER-CITY SCHOOLTEACHER

*Our lives are defined by the choices we make.
Do we pursue money or fame, or do we re-
spond to others' needs? Do we pursue what we
think will make us happy, or do we follow the
innate desire to live beyond ourselves and sacrifice for the sake of others?*

God has graciously given us all free will to
make choices. We were not created as robots,
and our decisions shape how our lives will
turn out. But our Creator never meant for us to

use our free will to pursue a life of hyper-individualism. Personal autonomy looks appealing at the outset, but it doesn't come with a warning label noting what moral dangers lie ahead.

I believe the wrestling this inner-city teacher is facing is a holy struggle in her soul. Something in all of us tells us it's wrong to base our decisions on temporal, fleeting things. We feel the battle is between our desire to serve others and our desire to pursue selfish ambitions. Let's just say the teacher decides to take the more prestigious position. Perhaps she could find ways to invest positively in the lives of her peers as an administrator, but would she be more effective in being involved directly with young people who have little hope that they can make a difference in society?

Whether or not we acknowledge God, He has given every one of us unique talents and abilities that He wants us to use in serving others. Most often, the more self-centered road ends up amounting to meaningless existence. Maybe this sounds harsh to you, but let me explain.

John Ehrlichman was Nixon's right-hand man on domestic policy. I respected John and found him to be one of the easier people to work with in the Nixon administration. We were both lawyers and naturally clicked. Like me, John was involved in the Watergate scandal.

During his trial, John's life began to unravel, and he was unable to make sense of all that had transpired. He became embittered, had an affair, and lost his marriage in the process. When John went to prison, I tried to keep in touch with him. Although I never had to testify against him in the course of the Watergate investigations, John resented me for being honest about his role in the crime committed.

After he was released from prison, Ehrlichman wrote several books about Watergate. Again, I wanted to keep contact with him, knowing he needed the peace I had come to know through my faith. John later decided to make a film about Watergate. This project was in a sense his plea for forgiveness. Although he kept trying to undo what had been done, his soul was never satisfied. In the late 1990s, I received a call from one of John's friends, Patricia Talmadge. She told me he was seriously ill and that his family was not around for support. I went to see him and found him sitting alone in his wheelchair. Startled by how much he had failed physically, I was struck with deep compassion for him. We had a long conversation. We talked some about his family, avoiding the topic of his third wife. I shared with him some of my activities and how my faith gave my life meaning and purpose.

John confessed to me that his doctor told him he could end it all with a shot of morphine. "Nobody cares about me anyway. Why should I stay alive? Tell me. Why should I stay alive?"

I knew a life was hanging in the balance. Cold chills raced down my spine as I thought about what answer I could give him. I told him that his life was not his own, that it was a gift from God. I assured him that his life was created in God's own image, which gave him an innate dignity, a dignity unaffected by circumstances. I reminded him that he owed it to his children to care for his own life. He would be setting a terrible example for them if he ended his life. I told him that he could know his Creator intimately in the time that remained to him, that he could have a relationship with God and even experience joy, despite his suffering.

I don't know how much my words affected him, but he did choose not to take the injection of morphine. Through the years, John allowed Watergate to define him. Like John, our tendency is to depend on our careers or jobs for happiness. But living the good life really begins when we understand this paradox: When we set out to live for ourselves, to define ourselves by what we do, we find only futility. It is only when we discover that our lives are not our own that we begin to catch a glimpse of the life we were intended to live.

**I HOPE MY STUDENTS LEAVE THE**
university with an open mind. I want to
help them find their own truth. After
all, all religions and philosophies
reflect facets of one universal truth.

—PHILOSOPHY PROFESSOR

———

*"You have your truth, and I have mine" is the*
*pervading sentiment in this era of post-*
*modernism. Loud, shrill voices in our culture*
*are telling us, "No, you cannot know truth.*
*Truth is subjective." In* The Good Life, *Colson*
*gives a compelling case as to why every person*
*can know objective truth that is not based on*
*cultural whims and fleeting philosophies.*

———

I am frequently asked what I believe to be the
main cause of our cultural decline. I am convinced the downward spiral began when the
Western world departed from its traditional
acceptance of absolute truth. Truth has become whatever a person chooses to believe.

Postmodernism has radically departed from Western civilization's historic tradition.

Existentialism was all the rage on college campuses in the 1960s. This worldview challenges the biblical worldview, which says truth can be known and can be found in God's natural laws. The existentialist argues that ultimate truth comes from one's own understanding of life. Sadly, such idle teaching has not contained itself to college campuses. Polls show that 64 percent of the American people believe there is no such thing as moral truth.[4] Most people believe we can just make up our own rules of living.

People are now convinced that truth is relative, that finding truth is utterly impossible. What the existentialist professor is not coming to grips with is that his empty rhetoric is leaving his students empty and aimless. They are left to believe that there are no absolute values, just tolerance.

Postmodern thinkers have made tolerance the new god, at the expense of even common sense. For example, Dr. Stanley Fish, one of the most famous postmodern academics in America, takes his freshman writing class through a very interesting exercise. He makes them create their own language. Of course, the students think this is a lofty, involved task, and they are quite right. But fourteen weeks later, the students are surprised to see that they have created a sophisticated, precise language. How? Well, they have to use rules. Although Fish's deconstructionist worldview rejects any kind of absolute truths, his most successful learning exercise requires both logic and rules to work. So my question to Dr. Fish would be this: If "universal absolutes" are "illusory," how can they be the best way to teach students to write proper English? If he really believes all of this, then how can he bring abstract concepts and principles into the classroom?

Surprisingly, very intelligent people do not acknowledge that they rely on knowable truth every day. All of us use the "rules" of language to communicate. We assume the "laws" of gravity and electricity will function on any given day. The cars we drive every day are designed to react to knowable truths about the physical universe.

Even determined existentialists from time to time need to recognize the illogical positions their beliefs put them in. A reporter once asked the colorful California congresswoman Maxine Waters why she was demonstrating for abortion rights. She answered it was because

27

"my mother didn't have the right to an abortion."[5] And she said it with a straight face.

We live in a world where truth can be discovered—objects fall down, electrons produce electricity. Because truth is knowable, I can discover truth about the natural order as well as the moral order. I can know that taking a life is wrong. I can know that it's wrong for a widow in India to be thrown on a funeral pyre with her dead husband.

Yet why do people assert that truth is fundamentally unknowable? It is because our culture worships the god of tolerance—even more than truth and life itself. In the past, people understood tolerance to be listening respectfully to someone else's point of view, even if you profoundly disagreed with that viewpoint. Tolerance did not reject truth claims; it respected them. Today tolerance means that no one can impose a view on someone else or even assert a truth claim that may offend someone else.

In her book *Creed or Chaos?* the great English writer Dorothy Sayers sums up our culture's predicament: "In the world it calls itself *Tolerance*, but in Hell it is called *Despair*."[6] Why? Because tolerance believes nothing—and therefore cares for nothing and finds purpose in nothing. Without truth, life becomes meaningless.

Truth—capital-*T* Truth—is indeed knowable. In small ways, all of us live *as if* truth is knowable every day. Our task in life is to discover capital-*T* Truth and live within it. That's when life takes on meaning and hope.

**MY PARENTS SAY I SHOULD WAIT until I'm married to be sexually active. But they don't understand that my boyfriend isn't forcing me to do anything I don't want to do. Having sex with him feels right.**—SEXUALLY ACTIVE TEENAGER

---

*Our culture often assumes that we have the right to do what feels right. "If it feels good, do it" is not only the sentiment of teenagers but of many adults as well. Colson explores why that sentiment isn't as innocent as it first appears.*

---

What is the good life? Our culture suggests that the good life is doing what feels right. But there is a price to pay for self-gratification. Many young people today are sexually confused and succumb to social pressures because we aren't giving them any good answers as to why they should wait.

In our feel-good society, sex is no longer seen as a sacred act that is reserved for the community of family. Sex is recreation. It's something we do to satisfy the self.

But even following our desires doesn't bring us the happiness we want. A few years ago, the Heritage Foundation published a study showing a link between sexual activity and depression among teenagers. For sexually active girls fourteen to seventeen, the rates of depression are more than three times higher than for those who have not been sexually active. Sexually active boys are said to be more than twice as likely to be depressed as are those who do not engage in sex. And both boys and girls who have been sexually active are more likely to commit suicide. More than two-thirds of teens surveyed regretted having sex too early.[7] Teenagers are not able to find the good life when they succumb to social pressures and listen to their peers who are saying "Everyone's doing it."

Sadly, teens today live in a society that is oversexed. The media know sex sells. Television, billboards, magazines, movies, and the Internet focus on sex. They don't, of course, tell the stories of unwanted pregnancies, sexually transmitted diseases, broken hearts, and betrayal. Teens are left with only the vaguest idea of what sex is really all about. Our culture is not willing to admit that sex is more than a physical act, that it has moral, emotional, and spiritual dynamics.

The fundamental problem is one of worldview. Do we believe we are here by accident and life has no transcendent moral law, or do we believe we were designed by a loving Creator who has given us healthy boundaries that were established for our well-being? Sex was not created for one person to consume another person as a source of satisfaction. This view of sexuality leads only to grave despair and loneliness.

Those who are trying to find the good life through sexual pleasure have hit on something: The physical act of sexuality is the most intense form of intimacy known to humanity. Through the act of sex, a husband and wife experience a unique oneness that points to something beyond this world.

**I'M FIVE MONTHS PREGNANT,
and I just learned that the baby has
Down syndrome. My husband is
pressuring me to end the pregnancy,
but I'm not sure that is the right thing
to do.**—EXPECTANT MOTHER

*The impressive strides of biotechnology con-
tinue to raise questions such as, what is the
good life and how can we make it better, more
profitable, and convenient? Cloning, abortion, stem cell research, and eugenics are all
issues that can redefine life as a commodity.
Colson believes that, more than ever before, we
need to understand the incredible value of a
person's life.*

Nearly every expectant couple today receive
information about the potential health-care
needs of their unborn child. Ultrasounds and
amniocentesis testing help to determine if a
baby is healthy. Doctors today are more

inclined than ever to perform these tests for fear of facing lawsuits for not informing parents of the unborn child's medical problems so that an abortion can be considered.

I think of my own grandson Max, who is autistic. In my book *The Good Life*, I tell a story about when my wife, Patty, and I recently went to visit Max at his school. Max attends an extraordinary school where his teachers pour long hours and intense care into children with special needs. The joy that radiates from these teachers is an amazing thing to witness. The teachers are not there because of the salary they draw; they are there because they see the value of every human life.

I remember standing in his classroom, thinking a troubling thought. Why does the public education system spend as much as $65,000 per year to tend a kid like Max? He will never go to college and never get a productive job. I couldn't help but think of Peter Singer, the famous utilitarian philosopher from Princeton, and his argument that societies ought to spend their resources creating the maximum happiness for the greatest number of people. Singer would argue it is better to use the money for medical research than to take care of a child like Max. A chill came over me as I realized just how natural, even convincing, that argument sounds, yet how dangerous it is.

The biblical worldview follows a very different thought pattern. Whether a child is autistic, has Down syndrome, or is a genius, every life matters to God. The world of bioethics is facing many difficult questions each day about the making and taking of life. The issues range from finding ethical cures for fatal illnesses to finding easier ways to abort human life. The question is how we should treat human beings—born or unborn—and how we should view human life.

God is the source of life, and He created us in His image. This is our source of worth. Humanity reflects God Himself—the divine image, or *imago Dei*. The beautiful, the intelligent, the poor, and the forgotten all bear His image. It is easy to forget our inherent worth in the sweep of medical progress.

Decades ago Francis Schaeffer pointed out, "If man is not made in the image of God, nothing then stands in the way of humanity. There is no reason why mankind should be perceived as special. Human life is cheapened."[8] Today we see this kind of thinking in how we view the unborn and the sick. Without God, we forget the worth that can be found in each person. Under Hitler's regime, all state institutions were required to report on patients who had been ill for five years or more. Then consultants reviewed who would live or die based on a questionnaire. Those euthanized were the mentally handicapped, epileptics, paralyzed infants, and the aging—those deemed to be weak. Of course today's doctors performing prenatal tests would not claim to be following in Hitler's footsteps at all; they see their tests as merely giving parents an option to abort so that their lives will be easier in the long run.

But it is crucial that we examine the reasoning behind our medical testing. The utilitarian viewpoint would look at my grandson based on cost-benefit analysis, not his inherent worth. Yet if Max's life is meaningless and unproductive, then why has he enriched so many lives? Why do his teachers exude such joy? And why has he been able to teach me so much about love? Because every life has profound worth.

**MY PROFESSOR SAYS WE CAME**
from primordial soup, that life
happened by chance. I know he is
smarter than I am, but why do I have
this sense that I was created to
accomplish something in this life,
that I'm not here by accident?

—SCIENCE MAJOR, IVY LEAGUE UNIVERSITY

―――•◦•―――

*Science is fundamentally based on trial and
error and the rigorous testing of theories of
how the natural world works. Colson points
out that when science touches on ultimate
questions such as why we are here, it has a
difficult time offering any answer—much less
an answer that resonates with how people
live.*

―――•◦•―――

Where did I come from? Why am I here? These
are two of the most crucial questions we can
raise, and the answers determine what choices
we will make and what endeavors we will

pursue in life. Did life begin by chance or by design? This controversial topic is in the daily news as physicians, teachers, and scientists engage in the battle for answers. I don't believe we can experience the good life without answering this pivotal question.

In her book *Life and Death in Shanghai*, Nien Cheng tells the story of her years spent in a dank prison cell during the Cultural Revolution in China. During her time in prison, she longed to hear word about her daughter, who had been taken by the Red Guards. At one point Nien almost starved to death from her grief. One day she found an unexpected friend—a spider. Nien began to follow the path of this small, very busy creature. It crawled to the top of one iron bar of her cell, then swung out on its own silken thread to the next bar. The spider's agility allowed it to walk on its web with the skill of a tightrope walker. Nien watched as the spider framed a new web before her eyes. She noticed the uniform spaces of each weave, the whole of the web perfectly symmetrical. Nien was struck by the spider's architectural feat. She marveled at how small the spider's brain must be, yet the creature functioned like a well-trained architectural engineer. Had the spider come by its skill through evolution, or had God endowed the spider with its gifts?

Strangely Nien felt new hope by the beauty she had seen. Her spirits were lifted, and she was moved to thank God for the spider and all creation. Somehow the threats of Mao Zedong and his Revolutionaries seemed insignificant. She was convinced that life had purpose.

It's not surprising that nature would lead Nien Cheng to God. She was moved by the self-evident revelation that such beauty and design could not have occurred by just random forces of nature. The evidence led her to God, the Creator.

Most of us have had similar experiences when we look at creation around us. Each night we can look up and see endless stars, whose brightness begins light-years away and attests to mystery and beauty. When the *Apollo 8* astronauts looked at the earth from outer space, they were convinced that only God could have made any of this possible. The vivid sphere shone brightly with life against the barren universe. From the small spider to the outer reaches of space, we are confronted with the evidence of Intelligent Design.

This question of purpose yearns in the soul of every person. Tragically, Intelligent Design is not being taught at most schools and universities. Students are hearing only about evolution. This isn't just a science issue; it's a worldview issue. Sure, it takes faith to believe that God spoke the universe into being, but it takes just as much faith to believe that the universe evolved from nothing, that it evolved merely by chance. There is overwhelming evidence that the creation is remarkably complex, pointing to an Intelligent Designer.

This question clearly affects how we will choose to live. If we get the answer wrong on this one, our lives are dispensable and worthless. But I'm convinced if we just open our eyes, the created order declares the glory of God and the real meaning of life.

**I'VE BEEN WANTING TO REACH** out to the victims of the horrible natural disasters, but it seems that any effort is just a drop in the bucket. How do we make sense of all this pain and suffering? Life is so fleeting. What really matters? Does anything last?

—URBAN AMERICAN

---

*Natural disasters highlight how fleeting life is and how easily our safe cocoons can be burst. Tragedy often elicits conflicting emotions—on one hand the selfish impulse to secure our own safety nets and on the other hand the desire to lend a hand. Colson shows us how tragedies and our reaction to them point to the ultimate meaning of life.*

---

It doesn't take much for people to recognize that our lives involve pain and suffering. No matter how many more waves of progress we witness, nothing can save us from trials. Many of us grieve when we see the disruptions of lives from horrific devastation caused by hurricanes, earthquakes, and floods. Some people blame God; some blame the government.

Can people who suffer still experience the good life? I believe they can, especially through relationships.

C. S. Lewis said happiness is found in relationships, and I've found this to be true in my own life. The most lasting fulfillment I have experienced has come from my relationships with God, my wife, my children and grandchildren, and my colleagues and friends.

I remember back to my time in prison. I was struggling with my father's death, being away from my wife, and learning my son had gotten into trouble over marijuana. The other Watergate inmates had all been released, and I felt very alone. Al Quie, a senior member of Congress at the time, prayed for me regularly, supporting me through this tough time. One day Al phoned me in prison to tell me that he wanted to serve the rest of my sentence for me and that he was planning to see the president about that proposal. I was humbled and awestruck by Al's commitment to me as a Christian brother. Five days later, Judge Gesell cut my sentence to time served, and I was set free.

I will never forget the hope Al Quie's gesture of love brought to me in my prison cell. The Bible says, "Greater love has no one than this, that he lay down his life for his friends."[9] I experienced this kind of love firsthand. True joy and fulfillment can be found in such relationships. In the wake of disasters such as hurricanes, earthquakes, forest fires, and floods, we have witnessed as a nation the empathy others have extended to many—from those left homeless to those who grieve the deaths of family members. Something in us wants to reach out to help those in distress. The relationships gained through these tragedies speak to what we were created to do—love others.

One man who took a two-week leave of absence from his job to help hurricane victims dig the mud from their homes said he never felt more alive than when he was helping the distressed people of rural Mississippi. He said, "Life doesn't get too much better than this—helping others, making a difference." This man has discovered two of the key paradoxes of the good life: We have to lose our lives to save them, and out of suffering often comes victory.

People throughout history have experienced these truths as they fought against slavery and oppression, as they worked to rescue people from poverty and famine. When we sacrifice for others, we clearly prove that people matter. When we risk our lives to rescue strangers, when we offer food and shelter to strangers, we declare that life is valuable, that relationships are important.

The man responding to disaster victims in Mississippi was partly right: Life doesn't get too much better than this. But for me it does. The good life is the life given not only for others but also to God. The greatest paradox of the good life is that we find ourselves only when we lose ourselves in God.

More than three decades ago I gave up my self-centered life and surrendered myself unreservedly to God. That was the beginning of the greatest journey I believe any person can have. I believe the good life is possible only when we are genuinely searching for capital-$T$ Truth. That Truth gives my life meaning and purpose now. Why? Because I know this life isn't the end but rather a glimpse of the beginning of our eternal existence with God.

Life is short and fleeting. There's no time to waste on futile pursuits of versions of the good life that our culture sells. Blaise Pascal, the great French philosopher and mathematician, once said there are only two kinds of people:

seekers and nonseekers. Either we are pilgrims, filled with wonder about our world, looking for real answers, or we are wanderers, easily distracted from what's meaningful and lasting in life. My hope and prayer are that you will persevere in the search for what's true . . . and find what you are searching for.

# CONCLUSION

You are not here by accident. Your life matters to God and to others. Life really is worth living. After reading this booklet, maybe you are still grappling with such assertions. Do you consider yourself a seeker, one who is still in search of the good life? Maybe you thought you had some of the answers to life's big questions, but you've lost your way through the tears of daily struggles. If so, Chuck Colson's book *The Good Life* is for you, whether you are young or old, rich or poor, highly successful or just trying to find your way. This book is for seekers—seekers of any kind, of any or no religious faith. The search for truth and meaning is a lifelong process, but it's worth the effort.

Continue your own quest for a deeper connection with reality that makes life truly good. Read more about Colson's life journey and how God led him out of a life of despair to living a life of significance.

# NOTES

1. C. S. Lewis in a letter written to Sheldon Vanauken, quoted in Sheldon Vanauken, *A Severe Mercy* (New York: Harper & Row, 1977), 93.

2. Christopher Solomon, "Why Poor People Win the Lottery," MSN Money, posted at http://moneycentral.msn.com/content/ Retirementandwills/Retireearly/P89288.asp.

3. Aleksandr Solzhenitsyn, *The Gulag Archipelago 1918–1956* (New York: Harper & Row, 1985), part IV, chapter 1.

4. "Americans Are Most Likely to Base Truth on Feelings," *The Barna Update*, February 12, 2002; http://www.barna.org/FlexPage.aspx?Page= BarnaUpdate&BarnaUpdateID=106.

5. M. D. Harmond, "March for Women's Lives Leaves Some Women on the Sidelines: Those Would Be the Women There to Support Life and the Women Who Could Never Attend," *Portland (Maine) Press Herald*, May 3, 2004, 9.

6. Dorothy L. Sayers, *Creed or Chaos?* (Manchester, N.H.: Sophia Institute Press, 1974), 108.

7. Laura Vanderkam, "Sexually Active Girls' Lament: Why Didn't I Wait?" *USA Today, editorial posted June 11, 2003 at http:// www.usatoday.com/news/opinion/editorials/ 2003-06-11-vanderkam_x.htm?POE=click-refer; and Karen S. Peterson, "Study Links Depression, Suicide Rates to Teen Sex, USA Today, posted June 23, 2003 at* http://www.usatoday.com/news/ health/2003-06-03-teen-usat_x.htm?POE= click-refer.

8. C. Everett Koop and Francis A. Schaeffer, *Whatever Happened to the Human Race?* (Westchester, Ill.: Crossway, 1983), chap. 1.

9. John 15:13, NIV

To discover more
about *the good life*, read
Charles Colson's new book

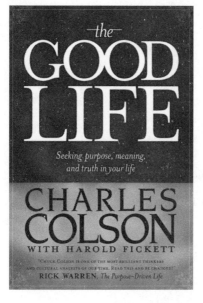

From his own life and through the extraordinary lives
of others, Chuck Colson paints vivid portraits of people,
examines what they live for, and evaluates what really
provides purpose, meaning, and truth in life.

HARDCOVER ISBN-13: 978-0-8423-7749-2 ISBN-10: 0-8423-7749-2
Visit Charles Colson's *The Good Life* Web site
at www.goodlifethebook.com for tools to share
*The Good Life* with others.

# Other Tyndale books by
# CHARLES COLSON

 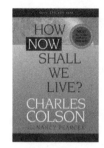

*How Now Shall We Live?* The classic best seller that has changed the way hundreds of thousands of people think about life, truth, and faith.

HARDCOVER ISBN-13: 978-0-8423-1808-2 ISBN-10: 0-8423-1808-9
SOFTCOVER ISBN-13: 978-0-8423-5588-9 ISBN-10: 0-8423-5588-X

*Lies That Go Unchallenged in Popular Culture*
Provocative examinations of the messages that popular culture propagates and how they mislead millions of people.

SOFTCOVER ISBN-13: 978-1-4143-0166-2
ISBN-10: 1-4143-0166-9

*Lies That Go Unchallenged in Media &*
*Government* A look at the dangerous worldviews that media and government preach and how these views undermine truth and faith.

SOFTCOVER ISBN-13: 978-1-4143-0167-9
ISBN-10: 1-4143-0167-7